For Dorothy Jones
from
Ross Garner
El Rancho de Obispo
July 18, 1993.

Donatus
and
Other Poems

1951—1993

Ross Garner

Cor mundum crea in me, Deus.

Binford & Mort Publishing
Portland, Oregon

Donatus and Other Poems: 1951—1993

Copyright © 1993 by Ross Garner

Printed in the United States of America

Library of Congress Catalog Card Number: 93-71799

ISBN: 0-8323-0505-7 (hardcover)

First Edition

ii

For My Family

Table of Contents

Poems on My Own Birthday

Nature Poems

Satires

Other Poems

Preface

It used to be one's excuse for publishing, "If I don't publish this, my poems will suffer from the scattering abroad of inaccurate and corrupted copies." I, of course, have no such excuse. I know of no one who has circulated any of my poems, copied, as they may have been, by the amanuensis of a great house, for the delectation of acquaintances and for the textual analysis and criticism of scholars two hundred years hence.

But what excuse have I then? The immediate cause of publishing these things is the insistence of my dear wife of forty years. She *likes* them! Then there are the fellows and the elders of my youth, the objects of whose encouragement would not, even could they be found, be represented in this collection. But by the time my poem, *Donatus*, received the 1951 prize for poetry (University of Chicago), I had been introduced to aesthetic and intellectual maturity by the late J. V. Cunningham, whose poems and scholarship became for me, and still are, ideals of what poems and scholarship ought to be.

There are innumerable others to whom I owe debts for the survival of these effusions. It would be unfair, perhaps, to single out other persons from the misty past. From the immediate past, however, I single out Marjorie Kirrie, a colleague of mine, who read the manuscript, and James Gardenier, of Binford and Mort, who has seen this book through the press with sympathy, efficiency, and speed.

Ross Garner

Lake Oswego, Oregon, 1993

Donatus

The John Billings Fiske Poetry Prize for the thirty-first competition was awarded to Ross Garner for his poem *Donatus*.

Donatus

*Qui fidem a perfidio sumserit, non
fidem percepit sed reatum.*

I

O useful fetish, in the Father's guise,
   Fashioned by us, endowed with our contempt
   To scorn and yet approve our high attempt,
And to excuse the failure we devise!

II

Midway in his thirty and seventh year,
   In summer rain upon a city street,
   Donatus first perceived the self deceit
And saw that fetish was not father fear.

Action invades events that are to come.
   Wherefore, since chapel doors were open wide,
   Donatus turned within, and at his side
The presence he invoked but started from.

There, much relieved for empty pew and aisle,
   Donatus, wet with wool, removed his hat,
   And where the ghosts directed him he sat,
And with him sat the engine of his guile.

III

Though gone from sacred grove the sycamore,
  The oak, the pine, the cedar, gone are they all,
  Cut for the pew, the reredos, and the stall,
Donatus would have had them as before.

Or would he? For the harvest god though dead,
  Osiris cut to pieces by the flail,
  Christ crucified and pierced by spear and nail,
In spring is brought to life again, he said.

Who is the Resurrection and the Life?
  Who not, if we believe with half our being!
  The image in the brain is of our seeing,
The sacrificial lamb is for our knife.

This effigy, therefore, to Whom we bow,
  Erected of ourselves to bear our sin,
  By which, what die be cast, we can but win,
Is all the Christ a good God need allow.

IV

But look not closely at the effigy;
  Think not to peer into the innocence.
  The sane man's phantom and the madman's sense
Alike are shattered by reality.

The sane have schemes to make the madmen whole,
  Let viscera be all the heart and brain,
  The passion fruitful and the duty vain,
Escape from mind the reason and the goal;

Let action justify its own intent,
    The origins whereof are buried streams
    That rise to conciousness alone in dreams,
Deny a choice, and leave one innocent;

Let *where* and *when* be government of act,
    Oneself the product of the place and time,
    Which two alone are guilty of the crime,
Oneself, therefore, the victim of the fact;

And let the Good be equal to the Bad,
    As symptoms of a superstitious wit :—
    The sane have schemes. Indeed one might submit,
If schemes already had not made one mad.

V

Force back the effigy into its type.
    Even the blind envision what is not.
    The double figures blur, escape, and blot.
Force into one the double center stripe.

The images have merged, *Donatus* said,
    The effigy, the type; the range is known,
    Not simply of the sighted thing alone
But of the point from which the dial is read.

We find by sight the point where we would be,
    It constant; and we, variable, move
    Beyond ourselves, advancing on to prove
First type, and after type, eternity.

The Father found, oneself is also found;
    And one once found, one is no longer one,
    For one is two, or three, and also none,
And self is lost to which the self is bound.

By which *Donatus*, knowing what he knew,
    A thing which he had never thought to know,
    Glanced at the chapel walls and rose to go,
But stood awhile beside the empty pew.

Devotional Poems

The Funnel

The funnel reaches down,
    Down through my skull,
    Its open mouth
    Agape to sky,
    Its slender tip
Imbedded in the shards of flint
    That once made up my heart.

I kneel erect to keep the funnel plumb
That not one drop of balm the Holy Ghost
    May pour to comfort me be wasted
    For a canted, careless angle.

What hammer could have shattered my hard heart?
What mallet was it drove the funnel down?
How can God's grace, in gentleness and love,
    Have done such butchery?

I wait in breathless, silent gratitude
    A new-made heart.
        O God, fulfill
    As now seems best for thee, my hope,
And help me ever keep the funnel clear.

El Rancho del Obispo
July 12, 1989

Dies Irae

The grace whereby the wicked thrive
    Seems to be thrust on me;
The wrath whereby the righteous grieve
    Withheld unmercif'ly.

The temporal of well is ill;
    To die is to be born;
And I am of the wicked till
    God set His devils on.

The Funeral

The spirit has no space but time
Now that the body's dead.
For substance is but pantomime
And spirit posited.

Yet close to where the body lies
Unworthy to be wept
The spirit looks (but has no eyes)
To see what watch is kept.

It looks (but has no eyes) to see
The pageantry of grief;
And every mourner's privacy
Persuades to this belief.

And when the spirit's house that's dead
Is put back in its clay
The house its house had habited
Becomes the spirit's stay.

The spirit clouds the mirrors there
As with a living breath,
Embodied in the darkened air
Perceptible as death—

Until time amplify the space
Between spirit and bone
And the dim portraits dimly face
The empty air, alone.

Good Friday

"My God, My God, why'st thou forsaken me?"
He said upon the Cross.   "My God, My God,"
I parody, "Why've *I* forsaken thee?"

Falstaff

Falstaff! Lush and lecher! "Fall on your knees,
Old man," said Hal to him. No doubt that were
The way, the straight and narrow way. But he,
Who proved to be a coward, liar, toady,
Pretender to a not-held power, un-
Regenerate sinner in the sickness of
The flesh, him we admire.

                    How can we so?
No doubt a wit triumphant when the game
Seems to be up! No doubt an appetite
To make him *Gluttony* or *Lechery*
In churchly pageants creates in all of us
Envy for sin that goes unpunished. Yet
Celebration of the very flesh, its glory,
Speaks not alone to weakness we inherit.
For God can turn our weakness into strength,
Through Christ, as Paul has witnessed that He can!

The Spinner

Outspent the spindle spans despise
To far more than the Spinner's eyes!
"I will a spate of wool away
To spare it for supernal day."

"Supernal day! Will that arrive?"
So asks the specter. "When alive
Spin out joy's plays in pleasant ways,
Spin out! Leave naught for never days."

"But ah," the Spinner in reply,
"When all is done, I will not die!
The wool not spun I'll not despise,
But spin it out into the skies."

Malchus

John 18:10
Luke 22:51

The wronger wronged into the right.
Traitor betrayed to loyalty.

With Iscariot, man of Kerioth,
The Tribe of Judah, went we garden-ward,
Loyal Jews we all, officers
And men. The will of Priest and Pharisee
We followed out. The Roman yoke upon
Our necks was done. The time at last had come
For action, prophecy at last fulfilled.

King David, God's beloved, knew to do!
A warrior he was, without compare.
And yet—must give us pause—Saul in the cave,
An easy victim of a just revenge,
Lived on to feel the burning coals in heaps
Upon his head. But Judas Maccabaeus
Showed us the all-consuming way to light,
The Feast of Lights! And now our time had come.

Messiahs come and go. But this Messiah—
One word from Him and Palestine was ours.
God with us, there was not a chance to fail,
Our enclave was our own. Triumphant was
His entry. "Hosanna," universal cry.

Foal of an ass! We thought it subterfuge!
War horses and to spare behind a hill,
Armor in plenty, Qumran filled with troops,
Captains of hosts, John and Peter, generals,
And Israel an arm that will rise
And old-time prophecy at last fulfilled.

Lord God of Israel! I knew not till
My ear was off, thy subtle plan for us.
My ear upon the grass, my wound a sting,
And I indignant but assured because
The trumpets now would sound the people up,
Herod and Pilate now forever dumb.
Our foolishness, we thought, would wake the giant,
The force Jehovah's mighty arm would wield
To bring Elijah and Isaiah home.

Lord God of Israel, whose property
Is always to have mercy, presumption
Forgive! Messiah spoke! My ear was healed!
The ear that did not hear, that did offend,
Was now renewed, heard now a blessed music
As never had it heard before. Oh blessed
Ear that leaps to do the will of God!

Lord Jesus Christ, the God of Israel,
Thou hast accepted me for one lost ear.
Restore me, Lord, in whole as Thou in part,
A sensate, loyal, living, joyous soul.

Praise to Thee, Lord Christ, honor and glory
Be Thine, forever and ever, Amen!

The Wood of Ephraim

I

Proem

New-planet metal jettisoned, we jet
And jive to our acquittal like the sun
Fissioning atomies, we climb the night
Through gyres of galaxies to flame on down.

But long before those blazing summer deaths,
Annihilation with the spring set in.
The blood and bone of Moses and his myths
Told not our substance where to stop, begin.

Our indistinguishable faceless piths
Are burned from clean-limbed forms of birchtree men
We could not find the fellowship of paths
Through unsubstantial wastes of smog and tin.

II

Absalom

Absalom reasoned thus within himself:
The tragedy is not the fact of death,
But the absurd discrepancy between
Means and ends, the *is* and the *ought to be,*
The whimper that is not a vast guffaw.
The antics of the heroclown are staged
In universes lighted by the cosmos;
And who can say excesses of grief,
Despair, and pain are not quite hugely comic?
Illimitable turns of everlasting
Thumbscrews bring but to wretched utterance
A comic yawp of praise or blasphemy.
Comic twistings of an eternal rack
Stretch a grimace but to a *risus mortis*
And pain can scarcely swallow down its joy.

Should we, mistaking our necessity,
Submit in cringing smiles and basely stoop
Fawning necks to th'ineluctable heel?
Such giving in is cowardice, or worse,
Acceptance of a bribe and mean concern
For scurf of our own soul, whose proper use
Is to be launched in some great gaping cause
Stemming in gen'rous, sacrificial gesture,
The greedy thrust of blind mouth, saber tooth.

Journey blessings

May God shield you on every steep,
May Christ keep you in every path,
May Spirit bathe you in every pass.

III, 203

But cause not just, the sacrifice were lost.
Just men cannot die in an unjust cause
(Wherein the pathos of the tragedy),
For heroism in th'apostate will
Is mere perversion and a grievous sin.

Yet who can bend the will which shapes his end?
The fight is to be fought, and fought with strength.
The soldier does not judge diplomacy,
Treaties and facts, ambitions, purposes
Which bring the war. Such things are not for him
To puzzle out, and puzzling, stop all action.
The knower has his will, the warrior
His sword. Be neither still, but flash to sight
Wielded by courageous virtue! A fig,
Fat fig to puzzlers and their paradoxes!
To act and to produce is all of virtue;
To love cause more than self, to act for cause
Alone is best. The acorn grows apace,
Refutes in its development the wise
Who hinge the cause of thing alone on thing.
Conceive development! No thing of matter
Propounds its end, its law, explains the future,
In its compelled round of growth and change.
The organism pushes toward the form,
Itself is cause: not time and space prescribe
Its bounds, which to believe is necessary;
And all material philosophies,
Cut at the root, collapse in heaps of jargon,
And with them chanc'lleries throughout the world.

Absalom argued thus: Those kings whose law
Bears no t th'eternal stamp of heav'nly form
As learned from God through His untimed decrees—
Which pour from the consensus of mankind,
Th'immemorial customs of the race,
The judgement of the elders of the tribe—
But take dominion from some plan or scheme,
Impose it on their people by the spear,
Are tyrants. Turn, then, to my father David,
Who often has transgressed divine decrees,
Not only as alone in sight of God,
But in a vile rebellion against Saul,
Usurping power, placing upon Isreal
An iron grid in which the common soul,
Its loyalty, confined, but finds itself
Truncated for a crumb, bilked of redress,
Deprived that it may feed the enemy
For hearsay peace and wealth it never knows.
This tyrant must not with injustice rule,
And I, who am so beautiful and good,
Languish with all my people in his bondage.

Then Absalom, with promises of justice,
Won to himself the greater part of Isreal;
And David, Lord and King and Father, fled.
But Absalom, who saw so much of truth,
Had turned his eyes from what he would not see.
Dupe to his consolation and conceit,
Worse reason's slave, not better reason's master,
Not Absalom would win King David's crown.
He fled and, hairhung in the woods of Ephraim,
Blasphemed the phantoms of his own defect,
Till Joab's darts determined his disport.

18

He says, "You've not dug deep enough."

To get into the deep requires to dig!
But one digs not from depth. One must begin
With surfaces. The deep, perhaps, by grace
Will be revealed.

                What are my surfaces?
A long life; much, much love! About long life:
Is quantity, the length of years, the test?
Ben Jonson knew the better part, *perfection*
Comes in little. Had I then died at twelve
I were eternal' blessed. For I felt
The stirrings in me of the Holy Ghost,
And said as much, almost! About the *much*,
Much love: how blessed in this life
My life has been, a long life filled with love.
And there's the rub! Betrayal of my gifts,
Of health, of brains, capacity to love,
Betrayal of those who loved and whom I loved.

Out of the depths, O Lord, I cry to Thee!
Out of my depths—not yet revealed—there come
Miasmas of mood, darkness, mists, as when
On foggy nights, lights blocked by droplets but
Obscure the more what was obscure before.
Confession have I made, both to the priest
Of God and in the daily offices,
And yet confession leaves an overplus
That plagues me with my guilt. What does it do

For me, resisting as I do, the grace
My Christ so freely offers? It is He
Whom I betray, not to believe, never
To trust, not to take Him at His sacred word,
Throwing His love back into His teeth.

How have I hurt Him! But His power is great;
Greater far can He be hurt than I can hurt Him.
Why do I not give in? Why not let the blood
Drain from my heart, and I faint, as I wish?

Lord Jesus Christ, my God, my Love, and my
Salvation, look on Thy betrayer as on
Thine enemy and on Thy neighbor. Then Thou,
Thou art in obligation, according to
Thy word. Love me Thou must, as always Thou
Hast done, and will do in eternity.

Prayer: Dear Lord, keep this exercise from being a
mere exposition of my rudimentary facility
with words. Help it to do some good, to be a
genuine exploration of what is going on in
my soul, so that when I re-read it—if I can
bear to—I will find in it a new leaf of the
cabbage beneath the old one.

Amen.

To Persons

Ode in Honor of Sarah Hall Ross

**My Grandmother, (1856-1939), on the
one hundred and fourth anniversary
of her birth**

I

And I, deaf by an ear, blind by an eye,
      Sit vaguely in a ditch,
      Peering at calf and buckram.
                I am ashamed,
And yet the nerve-end and its history
      Remain to solace art.
For to the senseless ditch on that dark road
      Through to the Now returns,
As through the glass of colored chandelier,
          The dining-room
      In which hot bread and tea
Brought the odd generations into joy.
          Spokes to that hub
Are all the elements of this my praise,
      For that its light suffused
The bushel of my adolescent years,
      The self-defeat of twenty-five,
      The inarticulate despair
          Of years beyond.

II

What though the rebel tear provide
    The eaten cake and had,
    The will parade its lapse
    In righteousness, and gods
Deify the ungodly. Borne I was
Down the currents of incapacity
    And even viciousness.
    The light remained until with death
It vanished and I did not know my dark.
        Day followed day,
        Each to be met,
        And this or that,
        And all the while
The universe disintegrates to rage,
    The years decay, and my nightmare cities
    Helped on by anodynes, produce
Gigantic and incessant mornings after.
    "Never got to the office."

III

The player scans the board and lets emerge
    Patterns of its reality.
Darkness and silence are but place and time.
        I have my nerve-end still,
    And history. I am not driven
    Down to ditches, nor escaped
        To rest; for now I find
—Where stand the Fathers and thy poets, there,
    Could I but see them, stand my years—

I have been searching still the source and gleam
Of colored glass in that bright chandelier.
How rainbow-hued the else
Blank, bare sarcophagus of pavement.
Into the limestone horror of the dream
Whereto my orange juice awakes!
What patterns in the cloth,
Sweat into ichor,
Hypothesize the end I search for!
Here in the nucleus of substance,
Disturbances in air to jar the gross,
Raw, unperceiving sense,
Is the accepted law,
The final, undecipherable red
Of self and twin,
Each all a moment everlasting,
Limited and infinite,
Centrally edged.
So fed, the stomach sighs its gratitude.

IV

No longer may I be defined by ditches.
Above the ridge, at last,
I try the murk
And *A or Not-B* is the past,
Paleozoic and millennium
Are lost.
Infinite speed creates a moment of
Infinite duration. Across the hump
The instant lasts, explains, and is.
The long light falls;
Unknowing can become again.

V

Filter thou gentle light and stained
Upon the island moment of my years.
For what was done is innocence again,
Hope is refreshed,
The Prophets and Philosophers
—They poets all—
On that dark road, their voices faint, light hid,
Throb in the sense, along the vein,
Pour from the real
Into the cell, transcendence immanent.
I hesitate, but can
I bear to enter that dark room again?

The Lover Admonisheth Himself

An thou canst not tell what thy thought,
As loving her in much or aught,
Do not then with thy forcéd charm
Bring down you twain to grievous harm.
But let thy reason guide thy will
That thou may'st have thy kingdom still.

Put up thy pride, then! Probe thy breast!
What course for thee and her were best?
If thou perceive thou canst forsake her,
Then must thou let the devil take her.
If thou perceive that thou canst not,
Twine round her heart till she be caught.

The Lady Ann

Out her tower she leaned and looked on me,
By that transformed, her knight all true and brave.
What vows I made to serve her worthily,
To cease henceforth to play the pious knave!
Too much of honor, then! Where all could see
She lifted me and placed me by her side
And made me first of all knight errantry,
"Knight among knights," I called myself—and lied.
And knew I lied. My armour was but stuff,
My charger good intentions, courage bluff,
And youth arrested age, my honor puff.
                    But let her not henceforth be the
                              less blind,
                    So prove me worthy, and continue
                              kind,
                    Who proves me worthy, were much
                              To my mind.

To Ann

This morning in the little car
You drove yourself alone to work
Through all that rain and cold and dark.

So once you pierced through cold and dark
And rain in me to where I work.
Such beauty in a little car!

To Ann, on Her Birthday

How beautiful, made so by grace,
Is thy (Donne's phrase) "autumnal face."
But Hugh would add this other thing:
Outward autumn is inward spring.

You are all vibrancy and sense,
All lovely, gracious, wise, and, hence,
My temporal, my Life, forsooth,
Is graced with thy eternal youth.

To Ann, on Her Birthday

Some there be who may deplore
How years fly by, as out a door,
Returning never, never more.

I fear no years, howe'er they roar.
Their heads, like mine, are growing hoar
But I am safe upon the shore,

With her I love, whose secret lore
Is able always to restore
My heart when it is waxing sore.

So slim and elegant of yore,
The more so now than e'er before,
It is she whom I adore.

To Ann

How gorgeously you do derive
Beauty from all your sixty-five.
But I, than you, am nearer Heaven,
For I am almost sixty-seven—

That is, if Heaven be my lot,
Which very likely it is not.
Then better Heaven here and now
Than not to have it anyhow.

To Ann, for Her Birthday!

Though years be years while we both live
And yours will not catch up to mine,
I would that I, intuitive
Like you, with inner light would shine.

To Ann

An Ode

No image taken: Icon painted!
Essential love upon this day of days.
It is the birthday of my sainted—
My she, to whom I sing my hymn of praise—
My hymn of praise unto the she so sainted—
The cynosure of all my gaze.

Visible icon: Inner expressiveness!
Sainted as earthly heavenness!
All who be must love her! And she,
Whom could she *not* love, who loves me?

Late One Night, to Ann

The FM classical?
Not to my mood at all!
I poured another drink
And sat me down to think.
Then notes of harpsichord
Ascended, and, O Lord,
No such serenity
But comes from only Thee!
From only Thee, from only Thee!

To Ann, on Her Birthday

Now what has happened to my lovely pen?
For I can't find it. What will I do then?
Just substitute this wretched object for it?
Ann's birthday go unversed? No. I deplore it!

Let then my wretched scrawl record her youth,
Her beauty, loyalty, and brains and truth,
And let no tennis buff reproach her game
Who's played on men's teams, nor her gem-like flame.

As we below pledge her undying love
Rejoice with Ann, you heavenly hosts above.
You are no fiction, fairy tale deception,
But as you know, Ann images perfection!

For Ann

The tinier these opals are
        They'll better fit thine ear,
Reflecting light most prettily
        Not of themselves, but thee.

To Ann, away on a Journey

Now finely drawn the subtle wire
  Attenuates to very woe;
But subject to electric fire,
  The less its mass the more its glow.

Those Unheard Are Sweeter

Like as two snails whose timid horns
    Explore the atmosphere between,
Us ev'ry slight vibration warns
    The thing unsaid is what we mean.

The thing unsaid is what we mean,
    For nothing vulgar as a word
Can filter spectrums never seen,
    Transmit vibrations never heard.

Vibrations never heard by ear
    Find ways into the subtle brain
And, unmistakable, appear
    Along the bone, the nerve, the vein.

For Noni, an Ode

My long-lost girl, a pledge of former love
                    Returned.
    And she fulfilled for me,
            As I for her
Dreams until then, inchoate, lost,
        And I rejoiced as she,
                Newly awake,
    So burgeoned, glorious.

    She now has found her way
    Untrammelled by a dream;
            The way's her own.
    And while I feel her loss again,
    I cannot but rejoice
    For all the goodness of that life I love.

To David,

aged three years, ten months

Vibrato, raging, headlong, and incessant
    You dash, tear topspeed—
    Clang-clang, whistle, whee—
Up down, sidewalk, backyard, lawn—
Fire-truck, locomotive, jet,
Peter or the wolf (never grandfather)—
All apostate elbow or knee,
Full of a darting free intelligence,
Not to be lifted up, held down, cleaned at,
    Smoothed or kissed or fed until
The pulsing pressure dims and weariness
    Allows replenishment.
Now parents change from worse than useless clogs
To heaven, well-springs, comfort-centered dews;
    Then reluctantly
You give in to the loosing hold of sleep.

For David, an Ode

Do not the saints report,
"The Father sanctifies the Son"?
We earthly fathers, types of Him,
Not by mere metaphor
Do truly act
The love of the Most High,
Have so begot our sons, without beginning—
But they, like as King David's Lord,
Are Lords of their begettors.
We fathers, then,
Are resurrected twice:
In us, and in our sons.

For Margaret, An Ode

I

The baby girl has now surpassed us all!
    The child who saw we had no clothes
        Becomes companion,
        Repays with grace.

II

    And we, whose child she is,
        See her depart
Complete, unto a life to be completed.
    Our loss bespeaks the time,
  And yet there is no other course
        For her,
        For us,
Fulfillment be to us for her!
    Thanks be to God!

For Margaret

What you and I do best, who knows? But it
Seems natural when funky blues inhibit
To do two irreconcilables at once.
The first is find in all that's inner an
Inviolate, unneedful self.
                       Yet flight
To the poor diaphragm, as that must be,
The very refuge found within the self
That looks upon the outer world with tel-
Escopic eyes as from some center nerve,
Proves but a dialectic of the sense.
For what is that from which we do recoil?
Certain, it is stronger far than we,
Else we'd not scurry so into the den
Of our own consciousness, as though it all
Were solipsistic nightmare? If the rout
Were truly but a sidestep to defeat,
We would do well to fend off life at its
Beginning, turning back upon the loving
Giver of All Good—that is, our Life
Rooted in Love (whatever parody
Of all that's sacred seems to color social
Intercourse), and like Caliban,
To curse our benefactor with the words our Ben-
Efactor has been loving so to teach.

For we must apprehend the other and
So lose ourselves that we become a *they*
And when we turn again unto ourselves
We may then be infinitude of self.

There are so few that know this to be true,
It sometimes irks us to be me, and you.

For J. H., an Ode

I

A tree there was. The blossoms on her bough
Made redolent the world,
And honey seekers,
In all their kinds, thence flew
And buzzed and crept,
And were sustained as by supernal frankincense...

II

That tree is naught but blossom now,
Whereto our sense resorts
As if that we were she,
A sacrifice we cannot understand.
But while
Her inner life remains,
We rage for her against the tyranny,
And yet we love Who first loved us, though
Him we do not know.

For J. M., an Ode

Our dunes evolved to meadow long ago,
       And we rejoiced!
But when there came to join us, she,
       She of the lace-trimmed alb,
Our meadow burgeoned all the more.

We heard the chickadees as not before,
And daisies tossed their heads in holy glee.
But have we truly learned to see and hear?
If not, it's *our* fault, and not *hers*,
       I fear.

To M. A.

The garments which you wore
Made tatters of my woe,
As rags are rags the more
That they are made to show.

But now out of your store
You give me grace for woe,
Your grace by this the more,
Your gain what you bestow.

Mark's Trumpet

The trumpet from the house below
Resounds a true arpeggio.
How far is *Bugle Boy* surpassed
And trumpet passioned out at last!

But in our house are heard the thin
If certain sounds of violin
And harpsichord. Let us rejoice
At three from two and raise our voice

In happiness and triumph where
Such music permeates the air,
And let all know, it's not in vain—
Gabriel, blow your horn again.

A Toast to Sandra

She's brains and beauty without peer,
And sheds her heavenly glory here.
We live below. Her sphere's above,
From her we learn to know and love.
For her, then, may this joyous night
With all her friends, become most bright.

For F. W., a Threnody

Today was fair. The sun, unclouded, bright.
And yet, how veiled, how strange, the Park Blocks were;
They did not leap for joy, nor clap their hands,
As I have seen and heard them summer long.
My long, dear friend was dead, was one-day dead,
He who had brought me to this pleasant scene,
Whose very presence made my passage fine,
Whose understanding lifted up my heart,
Whose talk honed sharper edges on my wit,
Whose scholarship sent me to dig for gold.

What consolations are there for us all?
Stays with us, yes, his presence and his name.
No doubt: But at the last, when all of us,
Our pilgrimage now made, what will there be?
One thing we know: the life that has been lived
To perfect verity, will never die.

Poems on
My Own Birthday

On the Sixty-third Anniversary
of My Birth

Abaddon bound, Apollyon spurned the gift
Supernal Love, that patterns Love extends.
But Edmund, goddess Nature's bloody graft,
Turned lust to love and thereby found his good.

What choice were mine, who now live parodies
So many years beyond the chance of war,
Beyond the deaths of many I have loved,
But short of the reality I owe?

Dinner-table talk of the Civil War!
A small boy joshed and jollied from the sulks!
A cane field where invasion never came:
A young lieutenant given a command!

Who loved me at the first, forgave and loved.
It was enough for them that I was glad.
The failures I procured to live upon,
They turned into a triumph at the core.

Hence, them I praise, by loving at the last
Who now love me as they who loved me then,
Those now whose lives are deep within my life
And manifest to me Supernal Love.

And in especial, she who from within
My life, by grace, makes all the vision gracious,
And asks for no return but leave to love,
And leave to mirror forth Love's immanence.

And these the offspring of our bodies worship,
Who now reward us with their happiness,
With being new and glad and all good things
Engaged in tracing patterns of their own.

Prayer

Oh Thou, Supernal and Tremendous Love,
So grace us that the little loves we live
In one another, truly, image Thee,
In Beauty, Truth, and Goodness, for Thy Joy.

On My Seventieth Birthday

Ten years protract Lear's three-score ten;
The King hauls back his crown again.
A fury interdicts regret
And if I'm damned it is not yet.
We old men celebrate our age
With tears of holiness and rage.

On My Seventy-first Birthday

They taught me naught: The years
Have done it, just the years!
But they— whoever were—
Were taught by me
To be
The sunshine and the rain,
Pleasure and pain;—
To be, the *years*.

On My Seventy-second Birthday, Being Good Friday

An Ode

"There is in God (some say)
A deep but dazzling darkness."
—Henry Vaughan

I love life lived. Receive,
O Lord, my thanks. But how I grieve
Thy Spirit, put Thee to the test!
Nor can I say I've lived up to my best.
Thy Son, O Lord, died in such agony
That heaps huge coals of shame on me.
How can I lift my eyes, He stooping from His throne?
I hang my head, exposed, alone.
How can I answer, when my day has come?
I cannot then be else but dumb,
Dumb as He was at Pilate's doom.
How dare I, then, presume?
He speaks:
Deep deaths defy delight.
The dark puts all things right.

In Spring, on My 73rd Birthday

Wells up a wonder at the will
Of trillium and violet
Of chickweed and of chickadee
Among these trees, upon this hill.

Wells up a wonder at the light
That emanates from who with me
Are closely fellowshipped in love
Till all my house, my world, is bright.

Profound the mystery this day
When in the winter of my years
The sun of spring and graciousness
Sends these and more to end my fears.

Nature Poems

Shadows deepen as moves the sun.
Dry leaves stir in a breeze that's dry,
And sempiternal terminals
Determine August afternoons.

A Spider Poem

A tiny spider, too small to
Catch me, crawled upon my
Page. But she was
Red, not fiery red, a shade down
Red to orange, and yet
Red.

       Would I had never
Seen her, too small to catch me!
Before my grace engaged me in
Her being, my thumb
Put out her light, and I was
Caught, not by the spider,
But by me!

The Gracious Spider

A score of length beneath the bough
The spider clings to filament,
In wayward breeze swings to and fro,
Can she be dead, or fly intent?

I wish to know. Take closer look
With point of pen just nudge the web;
She spreads alert, her eight-legged hook:
It's not a fly, but just a nib.

As she well knows, the clever she,
Created boon to all mankind.
I wish that such a grace in me
Would manifest eternal mind!

The Spider and the Moth

The rowans wilt in summer heat,
But on our deck, the flowers bloom.
I bring my work and take my seat
To make outdoors my little room.

A flutter stirs periphery.
I turn my head, distracted so.
A moth, wing-stuck-to-deck, I see
And jet black spider, cause of woe.

Head to head she strokes most cool
With fore appendages the moth
And walks away, to leave most cruel
The moth to flutter into death.

But I, eternal to the fact
Of nature and the nightmare doom,
With power of providential act
To save the moth from what's to come,

Reap benefit from the offense,
Reflect upon the spider's good,
Am privy to the spider's sense
Of moths and their destructive breed.

But then, this moth, pathetic thing,
Entrapped, his struggles soon to end,
No more to soar on patterned wing!
What duty do I owe my friend?

I give entangled moth a shove.
The moth wings on his way, scot free.
Both moth and spider have my love,
But one is need, one theory.

Dryades Cervinae

As when, one day, years past,
Slim and delicate, she stepped out
From the trees and on to the fairway,
And we, not having met before,
Fell, in an instant, madly into
A passion of sympathy and longing
Before she turned and disappeared
Into the world from whence she'd come—
So, this last week, another she,
Slim and delicate, threaded the path
From the trees up toward our
Deck! But this new she did not stop
To test my love. She turned her
Lovely cervine tail and disappeared
Into the world from whence she'd come.
Oh that she had trusted my faith
For an ecstatic moment once again!
But it was not to be. Perhaps
At some later time she will manifest
Herself again. I will be ready.

By the Seashore

Spindrift and spume are left
With wavelet lines of kelp,
And sand fleas lift their heft
Beyond the ken of help.

In muse and wonder left
So stand I by the sea.
Do I then stand bereft
Or is all part of me?

The Sapling Oak

My sapling oak grew straight and tall;
The topmost twig was bent withal.
I staked an eight-foot lath beside,
Entwined the twig to it as guide.

The second year the twig had grown
So straight I put it on its own.
Unwittingly I left the thing
Encircled by a piece of string.

The third year came. A gale broke off
The twig I'd not untwined enough.
No longer straight, but like a ball
It flourished till another fall.

Another spring and then withal
Another branch was terminal.
And now the scar is scarcely seen
To tell us what we must have been.

An Actual Occurrence

Black was the cat, with patches white,
    So was the chickadee,
The one, concealed by fern and rock,
    For opportunity.
The other flew down to the rim,
    For drink and bath flew he.
He bowed and raised his head in thanks,
    Oblivious to see
The hidden cat with readied flanks
    Who gazed most steadfastly.
Sprang up the cat, a bird-bath high,
But chickadee, more quick than eye,
Was safely off; and glad was I
To hear him chuckle in a tree.

Blame Not: an Ode

I

Blame not tree bark for fade,
For wood that withers to decay;
Nor say that just today
The pith was pierced
By nematodes.
If old be shrunk, their trunk,
Enclosing wherewithal to die,
Eternally is so.
Part not the dead from death!

II

And yet
Do not forget
The blossom's braggart bud,
Nor scorn
The lights of beady morn!
Our death? Our death shall die
In every truly living eye,
And life's love leave
Us whole.

Bush-tits

Twitch twigs of blooming arrow-wood!
Hidden from view, most deep within,
The bush-tits nip at seeds for food,
But on occasion one is seen.

So I, deep in my brush of mind
Nip at the seeds for nourishment.
But, Oh, would I that I might find
The meaning that the bush-tits meant.

Instinct with beauty and with grace
The bush-tits give me longing for
Such life as their so-brief lives trace,
They sinless to the very core.

The Stellar's Jay

It seemed, he sitting on the rail,
His crest adroop, his lowered tail,
His feathers rumpled, and his head
So rarely moving, that I said,
"He must be ill. Compare him now
With that sleek jay upon the bough,
        His crest alert,
        His feathers pert,
His movements all aware of *now*."

But then I heard up in the tree
The sleek jay make sounds new to me!
The raucous screams which brand the bird
Were not the sounds that now I heard.
A soothing "chuck" came down the way
To that rail-sitting Stellar's jay.
        I cannot tell
        If young or ill
But all I know, he flew away!

This October Afternoon

Leafy leftovers: Autumn blue!
And remnant flowers, pink and blue!
A stillness heard in inmost ear
Almost too beautiful to bear.

What grace there be to me such good
That feeds my life and soul such food!
But now lest I transcend my ken,
Oh Lord, bring me to earth again.

February

The chickweed blooms. Ten tiny petals, thousands,
All white amidst the green, and green amidst
                        The dead brown stalks
                        Of marigold, alyssum,
                        Petunia, ageratum and
What all! The chickweed blooms,
Cascading down the rims of planter boxes, hanging
                        baskets,
The New Year only one short month behind.

But one lobelia blossom,
                        Blue—deep, darkest blue—purloins
                        A chickweed's winter place.
How can lobelia live the winter through?
How can lobelia steal the chickweed's space?
This is the winter time. But were I asked,
What would I rather be: chickweed or
                        Lobelia, what would I say?

Eschatology

Death, judgment, heaven, and hell!
Here in a word is where I dwell!
A distant roar of breeze, the crows,
Acaw, the sun in facets glows.
How to endure the lot benign?
The love, the beauty that is mine.
A nuthatch calls, head-down a tree.
Can there be less than grace for me?

Borth Cliffs

Sheep on the sea cliff's carapace
Lie down beneath a spin-drift sky.
Down wheels a gull with alien grace,
The cloddy sheep all heedless lie.

Slim and proud to the cloddy sheep
She dances, golden feet to light.
The sheep nor move their limbs nor keep
Their eyes upon the wondrous sight.

The silly sheep, they chew the cud,
Stretched out upon the tufts of grass.
No beauty is can stir their blood,
Nor voluntary sacrifice.

In comic dance, the pretty bird
Held me, if not the sheep, entranced,
Dancing to music never heard.
If she had piped, would they have danced?

Nor seen nor heard, she danced her stay.
The sunny air was warm and soft.
All elements were one today
Before she spread her wings aloft.

A Fragment

I at my desk. Wind in the misty casement.
Wind in the chimney pots; the distant surf.
The silent little birds
Huddle beneath the hedge, while high in air
A sea gull rides the gale above the cliff,
Embracing all with out-stretched, down-curved
wings.
The little summer garden now is wild,
The sheep-fold on beyond is desolate.

Autumn

The falling leaves and silent birds in bush,
My hand shown parchment by a filtered sun,
Are so in distances of place and time,
Sustained by grace unto this latter hour.

Which compacts all, the kinglet and St. Paul,
Me and the tree long toplopped by the wind.
Who lives not in the bounty of today,
Ne'er knew the boast of an immediate eye.

Satires

The Amateur's Prayer

Oh Lord, preserve me from the
      self-revealers,
From those who write a line to
      show their egos,
What they are, their helpless and
      screaming little selves.
True poets start, not end, with
      all of that,
Take chaos and create a universe.
As who said, "In the beginning."
But true poets do not comment,
As I here, on poetry.

Two Brief Satires

I

The Stock Exchange

Presage pre-empts prestige.
The market's in a scare.
But age, *noblesse oblige*,
And, frankly, I don't care.

II

Lust

Lust, long lost,
Lasted a minute past,
But did not loose from heart, alas,
Nor can true love, alas,
In age, repast,
Lust's innocence!

De alequa administratione nova

Now watch stupendous stupors spawn
Stupidities of brain and brawn,
As though the glitz were but for kicks,
And fight and famine foreign born.

No neighbor does one not deny,
The rite rejoiced, eternal writ!
But poised and pensive prescient eye
Beholds the hollowness of wit,
And sighs a slight and single sigh!

God Rest Ye Merry, Gentlemen

Old, ragged, old-rag man on
              Christmas Eve,
His cart a-rattle, the steel-rimmed
              wheels a-rattle,
Roomy his coat and rheumier
              his sleeve,
Terminates rattle and flap of luck in
              gutter,
Extracts from box on cart a whiskey
              bottle,
Imbibes wherewith to soar beyond
              the battle.
      Spirit beckons to spirits, takes
              them neat.
      Oblivion descends upon the
              street.

Politics

Administrations imitate,
The deadly weight of them they hate,
The eye of stone that never blinks,
The ancient sphincter of the sphinx.

Compete or Die

"Compete or die" was known
To *them* but not to *me*.
Not then that I alone
Was silly, willy-nilly,
But that the stupid honest
Sleep all night long the soundest,
        Nor dream
        They scheme.

But still obtuse, naive,
I've learned naught from the years.
I let the schemers live
Amidst their hopes and fears.
They have their triumph's glee,
But what is that to me?
        They scheme.
        I dream.

Other Poems

My Stall in the Widener

The pictures scotch-taped to the wall
    A former tenant left;
The books the shelf contains are all
    My own recurrent drift.

There Kierkegaard mauls Sir T. Browne,
    Quintillian leads St. Thomas,
But Hooker, whom I've taken down,
    Has now to keep a promise.

The stall is full of light and air,
    Which gratifies decorum,
Most fitting Hooker more and more
    As *lux et aer sanctorum.*

And when I pause from *Polity,*
    The oak leaves in the Yard
All shadown forth felicity
    By Grace and by the Word.

If Hookerless this vision were
    Beyond my own poor reaching,
Thanks be to scholarship before,
    And afterwards to teaching.

After the Battle of Poitiers

(The King addresses the Black Prince)

Staunchest stood thou, Edward, of all knights,
Prince of the realm in truth, and I will grieve
Thee no more, but to the honor of princes
Put thee on, establish thee in thy raiment.

King's child, thou, predestined heir of the candle,
Ever to grow in grace unto the Kingdom,
Beyond thee lies thy drawing on, beyond
Thy darkness the intelligible unknowing,
Luminous and plastic to thy touch.
But far beneath the blackness of thine eye.
May thy spirit spin to thy Providence
And never die as die thou ever must,
But from thy marrow gather to thy head
And raise thy plumes in gorgeousness and gray
From iron blows and heaviness of sand
Till after come sweet savor and the dew.
Thus Crecy be fulfilled, thy glorious promise,
The purge, the striving bring the comedy
And naught remain but quietness and peace
Wherein are poured the gifts that now thou hast—
Save that, the fury of the body spent,
Thy waking part may through it all again,
Till all experience focus in thy heart
Unto that final everlasting joy
And death illimitable, earth and stars.

Soho

Turn

Pad wet pavement in American shoes,
Wonder at Soho. Try to embrace it. Merge,
Flow into glitter and opacity,
    Reel to juke beat and the assault
In conscienceless, improbable surrender.

Counterturn

Lemur life to the hypocrite waif in Soho,
Guiseppi, Anatole, Juanita—what,
What is it like to run a Soho dive?
(*Maria, ora pro nobis*, do you say?)
New York, Chicago: Satchmo lost to Mozart.
(The choice ought not to be disjunctive, what?)
Instruct the long hair, the too hapless square
    In the humanities.

Stand

A window mirrors the well-fed, the bow-tied,
Just off the Underground, between an errand
And the Reading Room of the British Museum.
("I would I were an Easter Island head
At the stairs' turning, only where it came from.")

Turn

The fit will pass. Durham and St. Davids,
    These Norman arches, will return;
All that power, elusive and so bold.
    So inner and transcendent is
Secure, nor all the obligation, doubt,
    Nor lassitude—nor corporation, govern-
Ment, nor policy, can prize him from
    Its gracious tyranny,
His liberal, most lavish servitude.

Counterturn

But now this pavement: hard-edged, wet with rain,
    The spring day early on,
From gaiety to headache in the morning,
Reflects the neon names of anodynes.
(Not *Thou,* O Lord, the people's opium!)
An hour left for truth, and then the pub.
Ay, there's the rub. The images of tower
    Facade, and nave, break up and scatter,
As though by pebbles thrown into a pond.
And yet their substance stays; the puzzle pieces
Within the marge belie the original.
Durham astride the hill above the town,
St. David's splayed below the citadel,
Pile and arch, mass on mass. Those mighty stones
Screen Soho in *montage,* and anodynes
Are filtered into sensitizing sauce,
Draught *bitter* into elemental joy.
Fulfilled before began this alien time,
    Twice alien in Soho.

Stand

For Soho, out of Durham and St. Davids
By the British Museum, is caught up in
The pageantry—her ladies ever gracious,
Her dinners savory, her wines all apt
And grateful to the palate like a burr,
Her people gently loving, kind, and good.

Chorus

So says humanity, and where is more
                   Of that commodity than Soho?

Typewriters, Katydids, and Guitars

I

But so the present moment be itself
In categorical imperative—
Offices and corridor and business,
The morning and me drowsy at my desk,
The flavor and the amness of it all
In sight and touch and smell—
Typewriters down the hall are *katydids*:
When lights were out
And I a boy
Was lying on
The army cot,
In at the open dormer,
Harsh, insistent,
An interference,
The katydids at end of summer,
Unseen in oaks and mountain laurel,
Shouted their presence.

II

The middle years are money-making years,
Before the slippered pantaloon, or rag
Upon a stick and head-piece filled with straw.
And here, past mid-career, retirement
No longer quite remote, not quite so much
An academic thing, the choices made,

The taught and lived-through,
Hoped and done and prayed and voted
Somewhat less urgent but more to be trusted,
I'd not go gentle into that good night.

III

Hence the guitar.
I who was musicless,
Fingers fumble a therapeutic chaos,
Intensity, devotion, fierceness put
For skill. And so it mostly goes,
An aging, faithful neophyte
(No, I am not Prince Hamlet).
His passion not quite frustrate
(Nor Polonius, neither).
Seeking in unaccustomed terms his grace,
But sometimes tone is elegant,
Performance in its kind excels
(Th' arpeggio clean
And counterpoint
In equipoise,
All belled in pattern).
And then the drowsy emperor awakes
And now is my Byzantium:
Typewriters pulse guitars to katydids.
Not that as so transformed discordant clack
And rhythmic rasp be recognizable
As what before fulfillment once they were.
But what Pythagoras and Sors both knew,
DaVisee and the other modest souls
Who play guitar.

IV

But I would not deceive myself:
Each moment is its own be-all
Because the act
Must seek no further end,
Microdisturbance into macro,
I am content when typewriters
Are theme and katydids their counter,
Drawn into music by my fingers
From strings and sounding board,
From tuning apparatus,
From nut, from heel, from bridge, from all
The other limitless perfections
Of my guitar—
To find in my guitar the ripeness for
The plucking, consciousness abstracted from
The dream, and brought to form.

My Violin

I love my violin!
It cannot be a sin!
I'd find it very odd
To worship it as God.

But when the sound I hear
Is music of the sphere,
The cow doth homeward plod,
And so, I hope, to God.

Name not my Name

Name not my name
In crystal spider webs
Nor tinsel trees
Nor burnished blossomettes.

For I have climbed
Clouds in exalted seas,
Escaped to other space
In escapade.

The seen seems ornament
And murks and darks
The substance meant,
And I have glimpsed.

In downward glide
Be now my heart alive
That I may not forget—
That I may not forget!

Blue-Suited Man

A cold spring rain and puddles in the street.
An early afternoon. Warehouses, wharves
All but deserted but for us and him:
Blue-suited man, umbrella, dainty shoes.

Is he some unemployed precisionist
Bound for an interview and gone for broke?
Is he a shake-down artist, small-hit man,
A contract killer: job first, then the date?

Or is he, bathed and sweet, enticed to rooms
Remote and hidden, where he's waited for?
And will what happens there then manifest
An inner grace, as now the mud-edged street
Has manifested blue? Blue-suited man
      That gives the street its being.

The Heart's Reprieve

I wait for what will weave
My heart its own reprieve—
       My heart
         That knows the art
Of pride and sense
And prim pretense
Hypocrisy's achieve.

But sacring bell procures
Layers of life, ensures
       The art
         To save the heart
From pride and sense
         And prim pretense,
Hypocrisy's allures!

The Palimpsest

A palimpsest of passage prods
My memory of men and mud.
But how the passing of the gods
To that beyond the understood
Leaves vacant my vacation time,
Void both of reason and of rhyme

And chaos clings charisma down
In faultless existential fault
And governance now heedless grown
Destroys the saltness of the salt.
How wan the wonder, and the savor
Until some god restores the flavor.

The Dead-end of the Lost Best

The developer—bad cess to him!—
Cuts down the trees, gouges out the
Soil, and is, at this moment, framing
Four houses in our back yard.
They are Norman French.

Would that we did own our own
Back yard. We would never
Settle for such pricey
Desecration—whatever the three-car-garaged,
Hip-roofed mansions may sell for!
Where are the truths of Louis Sullivan and
Frank Lloyd Wright? Our era must be the
Dead-end of the lost best.

But the developer who built
Our house, similarly gouged out the soil,
Cut down the trees, opened up to
Exploitation a virgin wilderness. And I
Could not wish our house *un*built. It does, however,
Fit! Our landscape is not Norman
French, nor was our north-west
House, new many years ago,
Expensive. However much its dollar value may
Rise by the showy structures in our own
Back yard, we will think ourselves in better
Taste, living in a modest house, where we
Hope to live forever!

The Habit

Starch, wool, winding sheets, straitjackets,
Drapery—I understand the discomfort of the
Medieval, habit-wearing, habit-forming garment.
But, Oh! the infinite variety of sense
And personality inside the armor!

But nuns in those early days were
Often seen, by ignorant, inexperienced
Eyes, as stereotypes, mere effigies, and
The *habit* got in the way. The eyes were
Afraid of hidden, arcane modes, to them
Concealing rather than revealing
Whatever truths a freedom may aspire to.
The pressures of suspicion and conformity
Have won.

       But this photograph—look upon the face of
The dedicated nun, in its starched frame: how beautiful
It is, the face in all tranquillity! Many hours a day of
Opus dei, many years, nay centuries, of grace!

The habit was, indeed, an outward and
Visible sign of an inward and spiritual grace. But so is
Now the free-wheeling Sister, showing forth the
Love of Christ, her every gesture, an expression of
Her consecrated heart, belying the secular costume
Which, she hopes, will make her look like everybody
Else. But I would know her anywhere,
In any costume—and I thank God
For her.

How It All Works

The chain of being slips the cog of chance,
Exalts us up into the cosmic dance,
Nor can our fate compel an end, and thence,
We know the mean, and it is Providence.

Envoy

A subterfuge of fake and guilt
Could now betray the house Jack built.
But let facade be but the face
And all the structure saved by grace.